Let's compromise-
and say I'm right..

Let's compromise - and say I'm right..

Calman on Love & Relationships

Edited by Stephanie Calman
Foreword by Michael Palin

Souvenir Press

This collection first published in Great Britain in 2015
by Souvenir Press Ltd, 43 Great Russell Street, London WC1B 3PD

ISBN 9780285643093

Photograph of Mel Calman courtesy of Alan Young

Many of the drawings included in this volume were previously
published in book form in the following volumes:

Calman & Women (Jonathan Cape, 1967), *Dr Calman's Dictionary of Psychoanalysis* (W.H. Allen, 1979), *But it's my turn to leave you . . .* (Methuen, 1980), *How about a little quarrel before bed?* (Methuen, 1981), *It's only you that's incompatible!* (Methuen, 1984), *A little light worrying* (Methuen, 1996)

Typeset by M Rules

Printed and bound in Great Britain by
Clays Ltd, St Ives plc

Foreword

Love and Marriage

We all know, thanks to Frank Sinatra, that love and marriage go together like a horse and carriage. Mel Calman, on the other hand, saw the horse riderless and the carriage overturned. His talent for using humour to pin-point our fears, anxieties and evasions was at its perceptive best when tip-toeing through that minefield of emotions that faces any human being who fancies another.

If it was as easy as Frank Sinatra told us it was than we wouldn't need a Mel Calman. Mel's cartoons remind us that life is complicated. That it is full of contradictions. That we are not good at saying what we want, or wanting what we say. Especially when it comes to attraction. There is something in the north European psyche that cannot easily deal with this awkward emotion. When it comes to knowing when to fight or sell dodgy insurance we've no trouble at all, but when it comes to telling somebody that we like them we're all fingers and thumbs. And there's not much we can do about it, but be honest with ourselves and not get too anxious.

Which is why we need more of Mel. It is not a distorting mirror he holds up to us, but one which is uncomfortably truthful. He shows us putting our foot down, but invariably in the wrong place. Making our minds up only to change them instantly. Turning everlasting love into long-term imprisonment. He played on these inconsistencies, not in a jeering or judgemental way, but with a wit and sensitivity that makes us laugh, ruefully as in 'Familiarity has come between us', joyfully, as in 'Free Women Now!' / 'Can I have one?' and with a guffaw of recognition, as in 'How was it for you?' / 'How was what?'

He had an uncanny ear for the nuances of self-delusion without ever making us feel we're being mocked. In fact it's the opposite. Far from being judged, we feel that we are sharing the confusion with the cartoonist himself. Mel was like that – a psychiatrist who makes you laugh.

His graphic style is minimalist, but it conveys so much. One of his great skills was to condense pretension and pomposity to a short sharp one liner, usually delivered by a short icon of a man, probably Mel himself. Occasionally there is some almost indecently busy action, all the more effective for being a surprise. As in the red heart being hurled like a discus.

He did concentration and concision with such a deft touch that we are sometimes given much more than we expected. A man in bed saying to his wife 'Being a failure isn't as easy as it looks' could be from one of Tennessee Williams' notebooks. And how about this for the start of a novel? Woman to Man: '*You don't understand women.*' Man: '*You never let me meet any.*'

Mel was an eloquent miniaturist. An exceptionally acute

observer of the human condition. I'd recommend this volume to anyone in love or thinking of getting married. Or, more particularly, to anyone out of love and wondering where it all went wrong. These wonderful cartoons won't stem the tears but they might just produce some choking laughter. And that's a start.

Michael Palin
London, March 2015

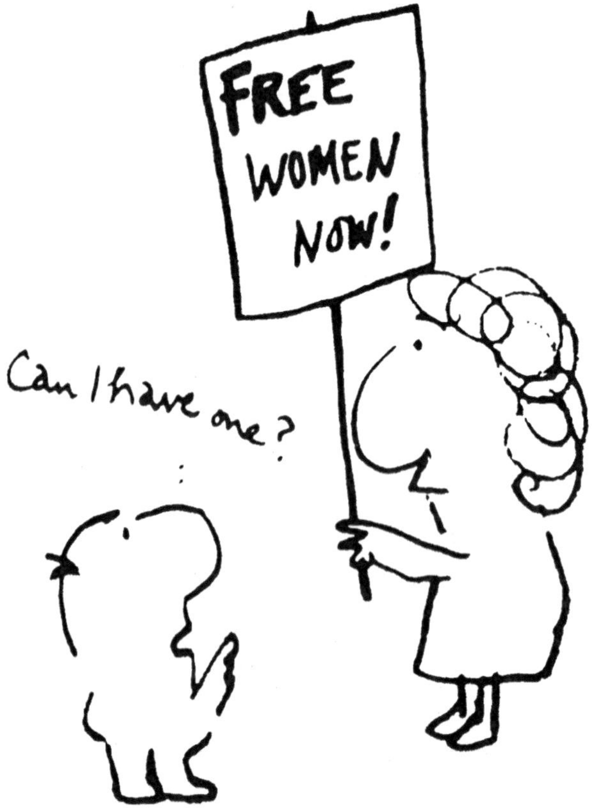
FREE WOMEN NOW!
Can I have one?

Introduction

When my father Mel Calman died in 1994 at the age of just 62, his readers missed him deeply. They felt as did we, his family and friends, that no-one could express the sane human response to a crisis, be it personal or political, so succinctly.

In his files we found many letters, going back decades, from people grateful for this or that joke, often ending with the remark: 'You summed up just how I feel.' Whether on current events, war, fear, parenting, food, travel – any subject – he spoke for many of us, and in so few words. But it was in the area of human relations that he truly excelled, and where his work is timeless.

For Relate he once designed a tea towel, featuring a man and a woman sitting with their backs to each other. The woman is saying, *'I'm not talking to you'* and the man replying: *'That's ok – I'm not listening.'*

It shows his instinctive grasp of how communication itself can become a battleground. My own favourite on this theme is one man telling another: *'My wife hasn't spoken to me for three days'. 'Perhaps'* says his friend, *'she's trying to tell you something.'* It's so 'him', and yet universal. And, more than thirty years on, it hasn't dated at all.

The same goes for my teenage children's favourite, a man looking up at a woman with a placard demanding '*Free Women Now*' – and asking, '*Can I have one?*'

And I don't think it diminishes his achievements as a dramatist of the human condition to say that some of his captions were actually taken from life. It was recognising which of those phrases had a life beyond the bedroom, or the kitchen, and boiling them down to their very essence, at which he excelled. '*It's only you that's Incompatible!*', which became the title of one of his books, was said by an exasperated wife – I had better not say which one – just before she slammed the door on yet another row. And '*I related to you yesterday – today I'm resting*' was his own, real life riposte to one woman's endless need for conversation. As he might have said, there is such a thing as too much communication. He knew exactly which sort of ridiculous things each sex is prone to saying, and one never felt, as a woman, offended or misunderstood. There are whole conversations, even entire relationships – albeit probably the shorter ones, portrayed in those seemingly effortless retorts.

Above all, he brilliantly zoned in on that paradox of love and commitment, namely that we fall in love with each other, move in together, marry even – and find that that very proximity brings its own problems. In fact, he didn't live with his last partner at all, as if he'd spent his life adjusting the distances back and forth to get just the right level of closeness, and had finally achieved it. But of course, the two marriages yielded the better jokes. One of the many collections he published during his extraordinary thirty-eight year career is dedicated '*to my ex-wives, for their help with the research*'. I hope they took it – and take this too – in the right spirit.

Stephanie Calman

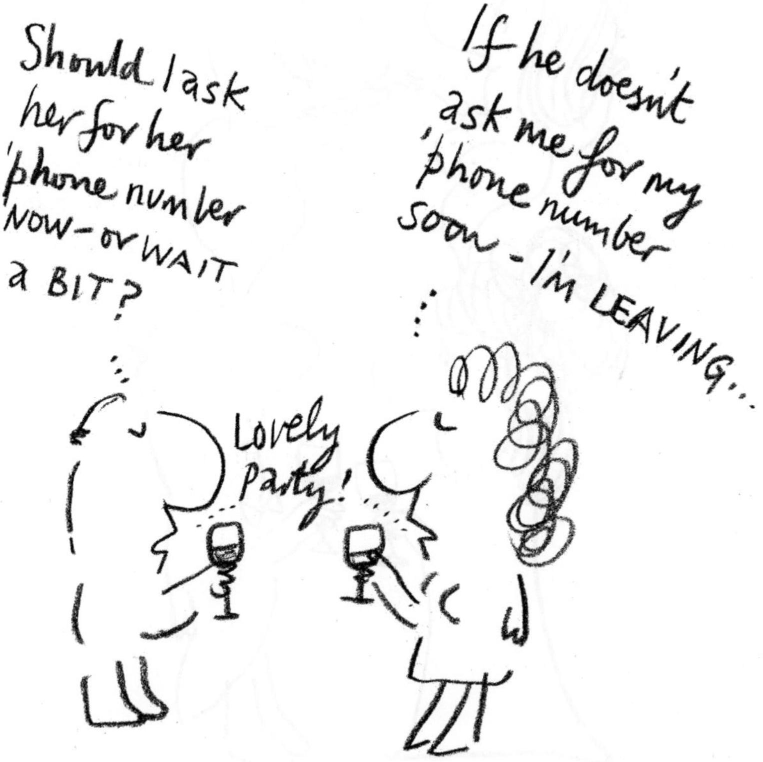
Should I ask her for her 'phone number NOW – or WAIT a BIT?
If he doesn't ask me for my 'phone number soon – I'm LEAVING...
Lovely Party!

Now tell me all about yourself_ briefly...

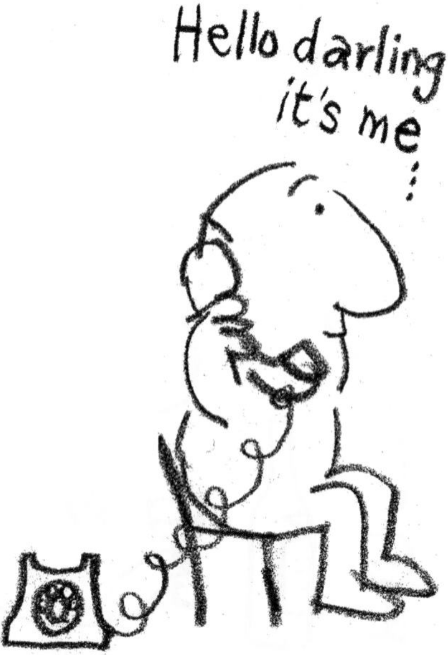
Hello darling!
it's me...

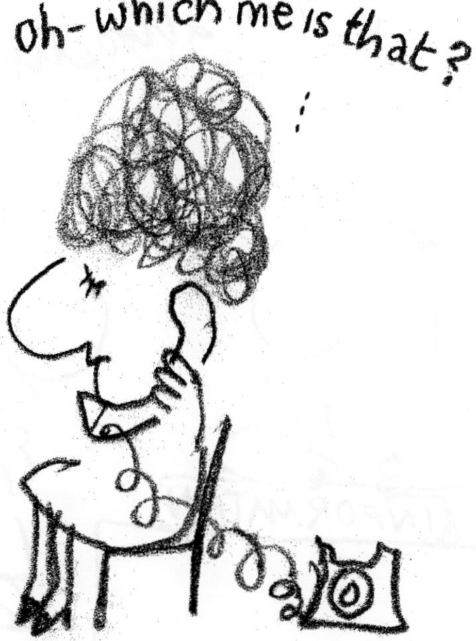
Oh- which me is that?

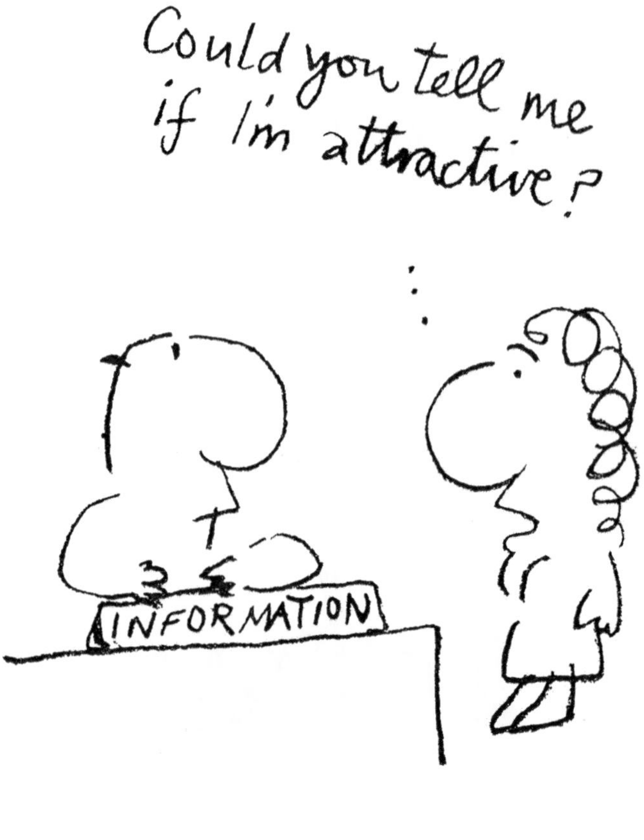
Could you tell me if I'm attractive?
INFORMATION

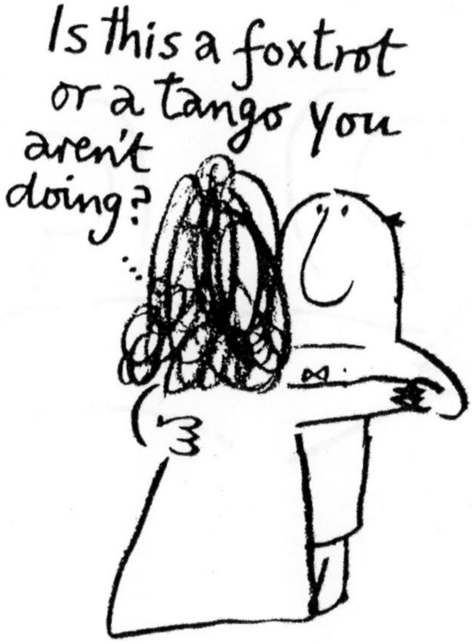
Is this a foxtrot or a tango you aren't doing?

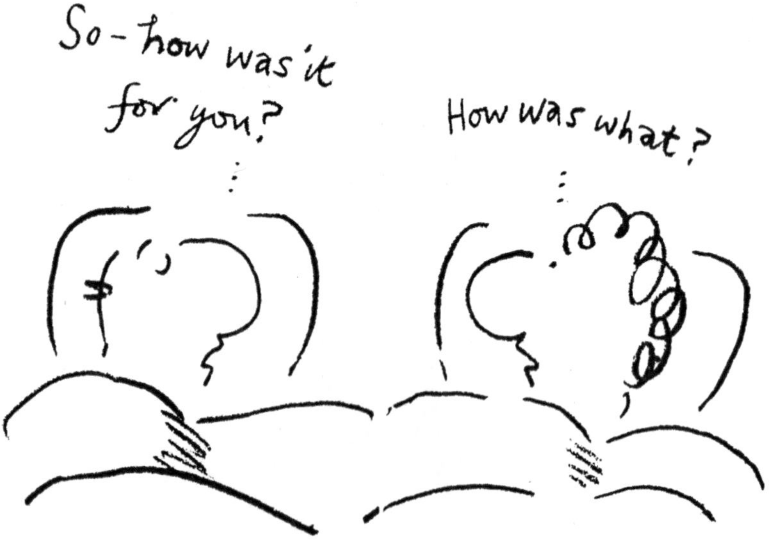
So - how was it for you?
How was what?

The last time
I went into one of
those it took me
five years to
get out...

Why should I phone him?
I ALWAYS phone him..
And he's probably not in..
ALWAYS OUT doing things -
enjoying himself..
He never phones me.
I wish he would just
ONCE phone me..
I'll give him five more
minutes and then
I'm going out!

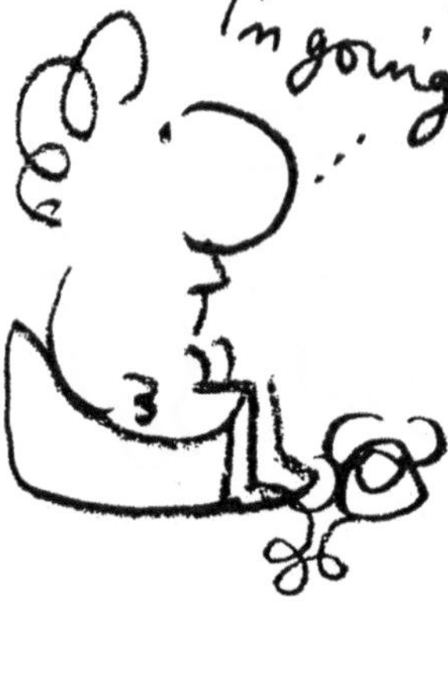

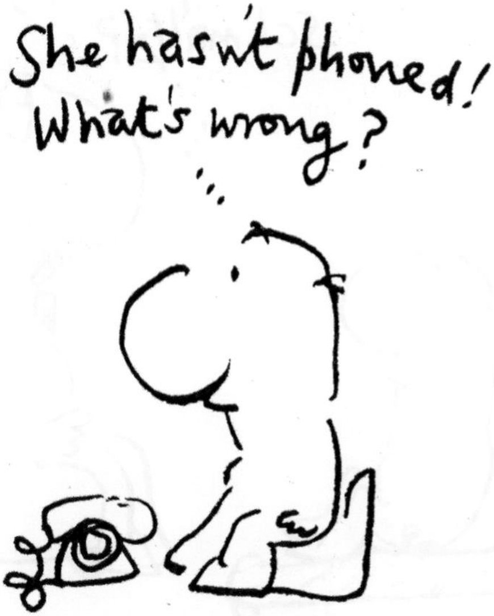
She hasn't phoned!
What's wrong?

When you say 'Love'
do you mean EROS or
a need for instinctual
satisfaction or object love
or oedipal love
or genital love
or simple old-fashioned
schmaltz?

When I say 'yes'-
I mean 'yes, but'-

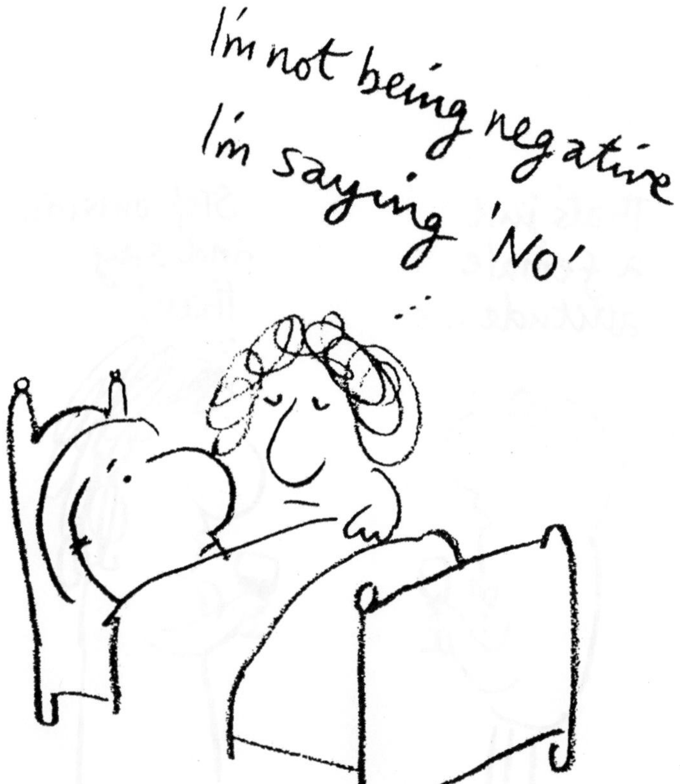
I'm not being negative
I'm saying 'NO'
...

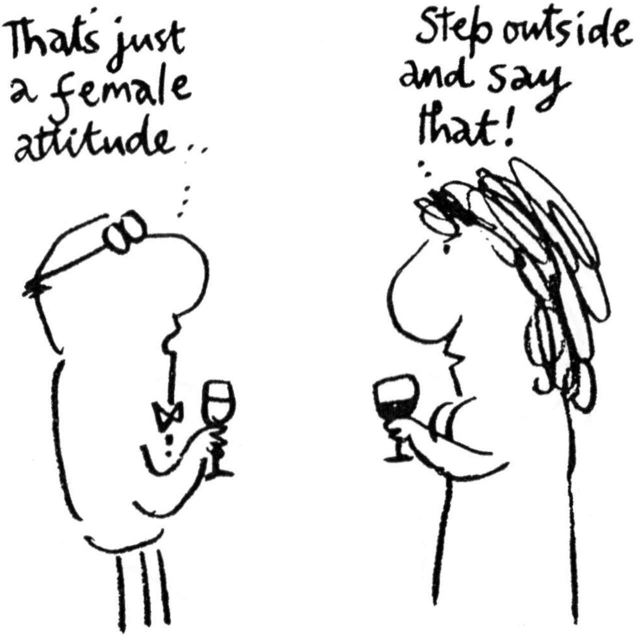
That's just a female attitude...
Step outside and say that!

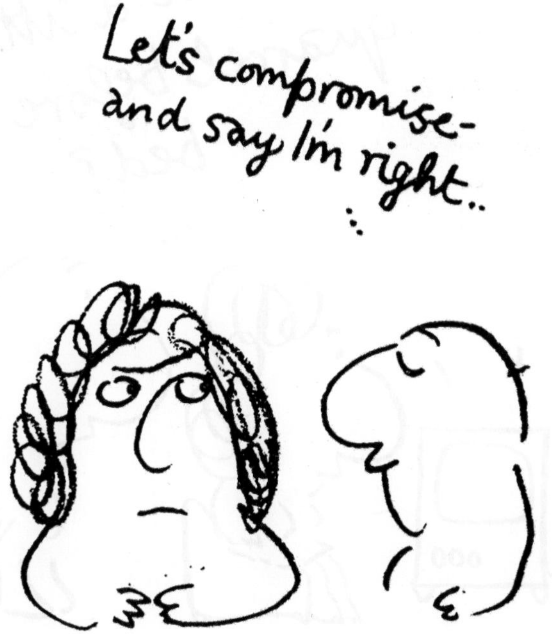
Let's compromise-
and say I'm right..

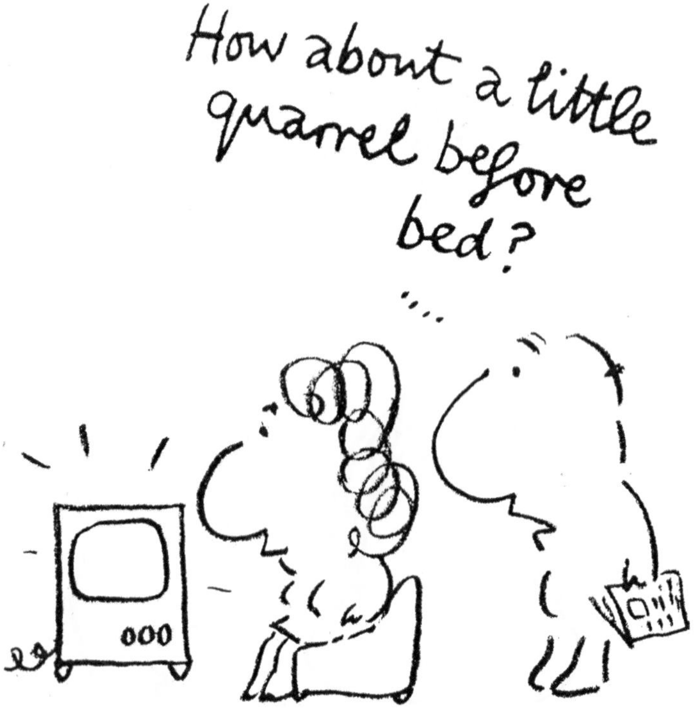
How about a little quarrel before bed?

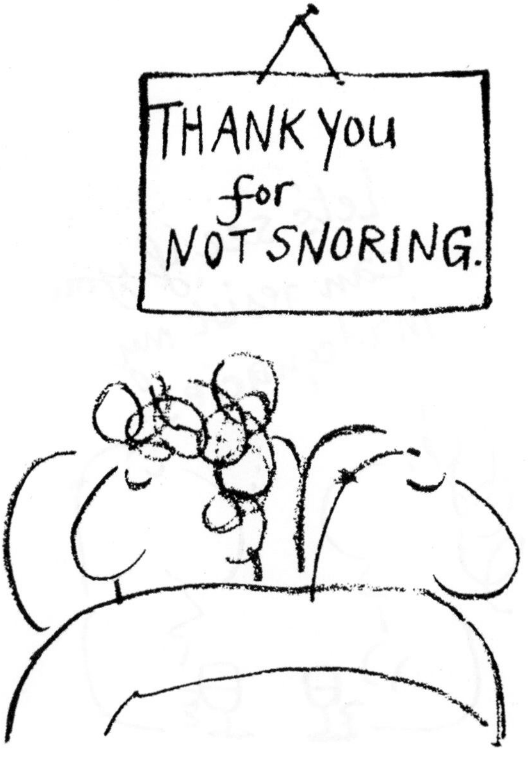
THANK YOU
for
NOT SNORING.

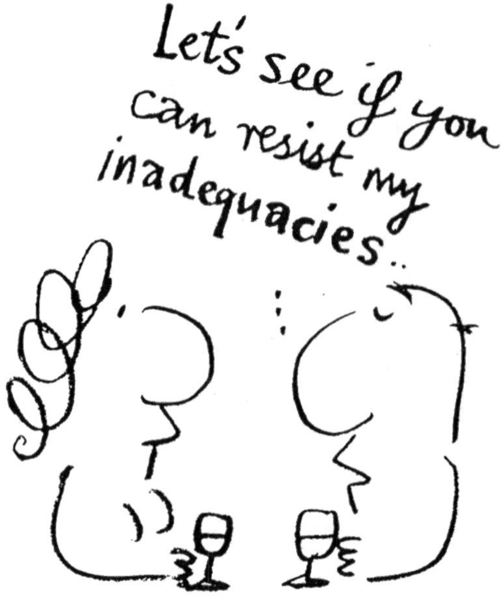
Let's see if you can resist my inadequacies..

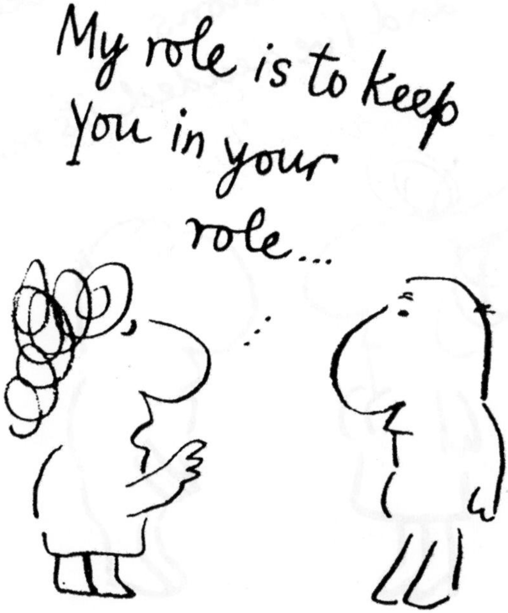
My role is to keep you in your role...

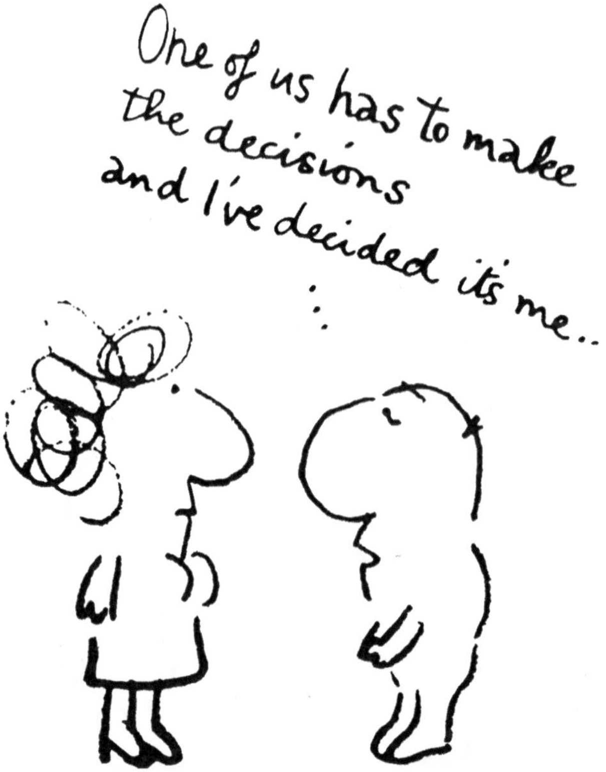
One of us has to make the decisions and I've decided it's me...

I promise to LOVE, HONOUR and laugh at your JOKES ..

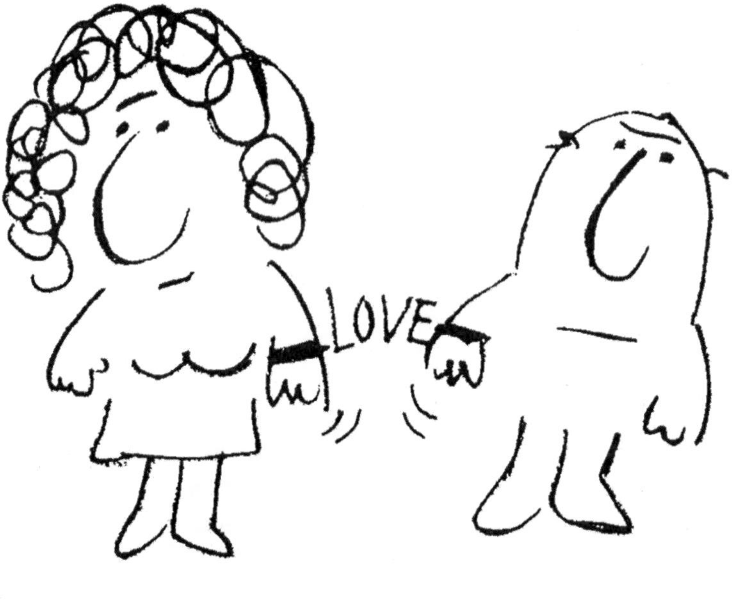
LOVE

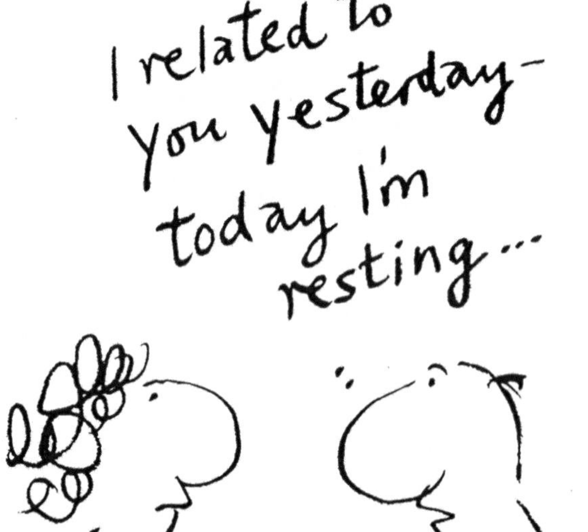
I related to you yesterday- today I'm resting...

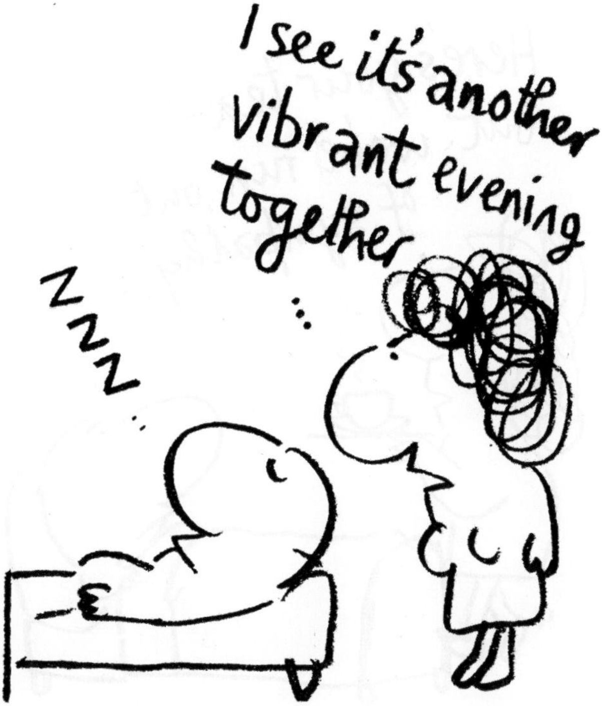
I see it's another vibrant evening together...
ZZZ..

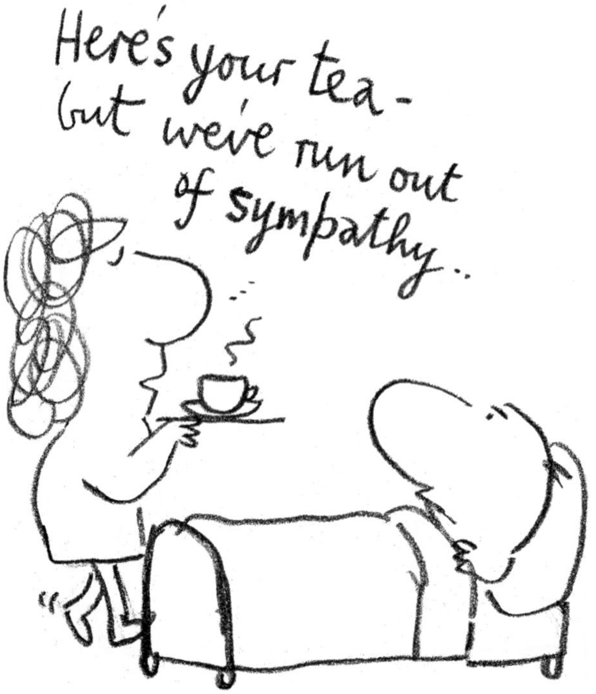
Here's your tea - but we've run out of sympathy...

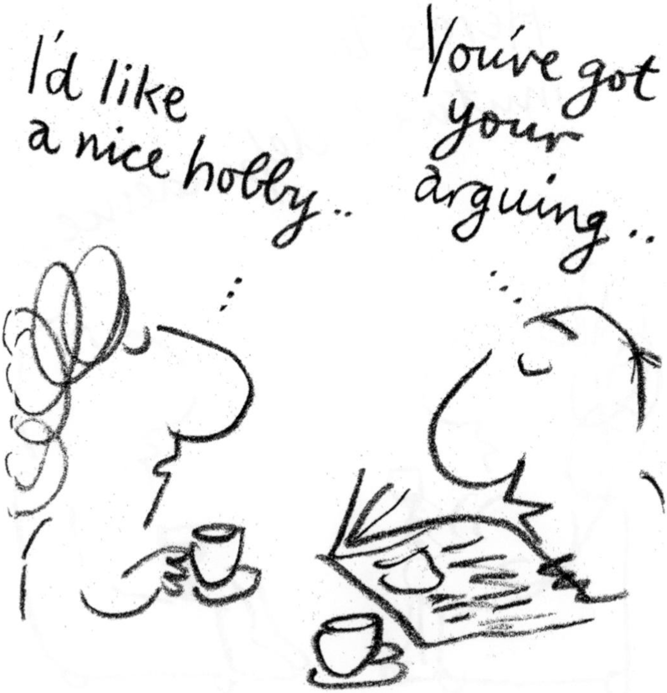
I'd like a nice hobby..
You've got your arguing..

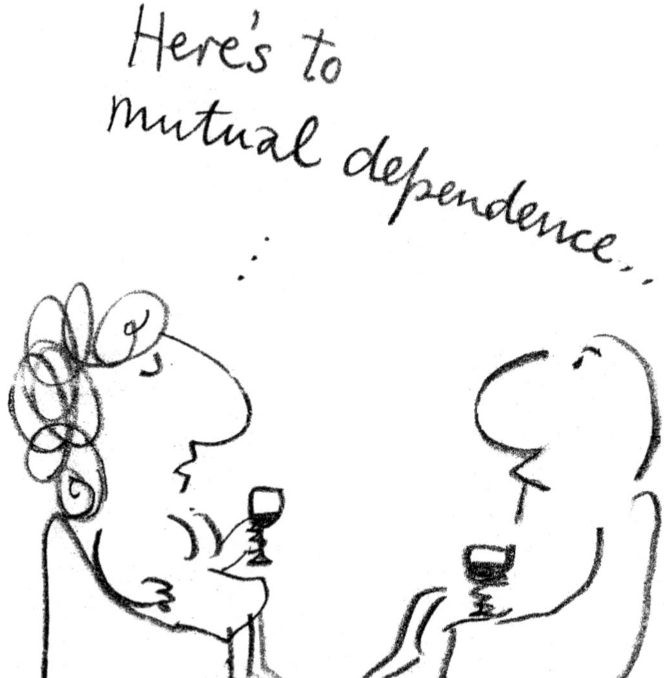
Here's to mutual dependence...

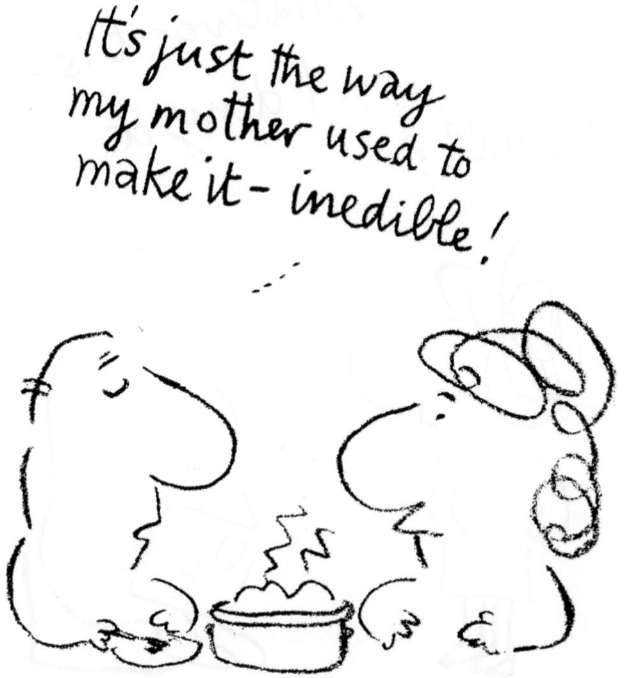
It's just the way my mother used to make it - inedible!

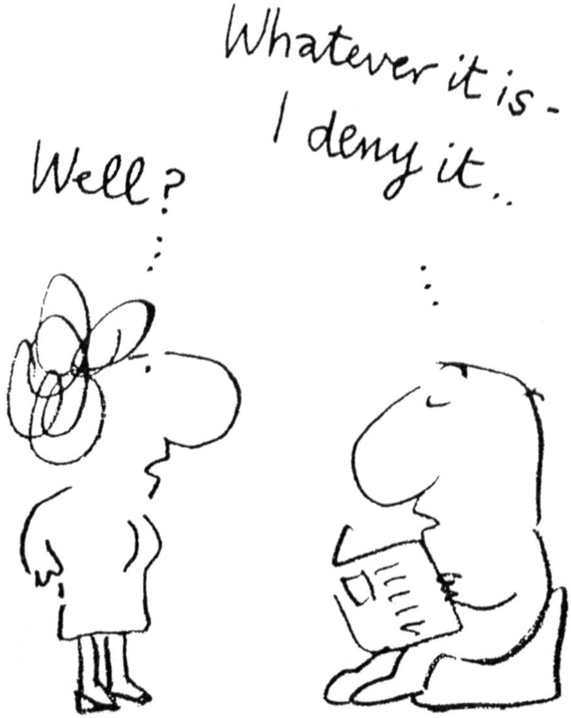
Well?
Whatever it is -
I deny it..

Doctor -
I'm suffering from
bouts of marriage...

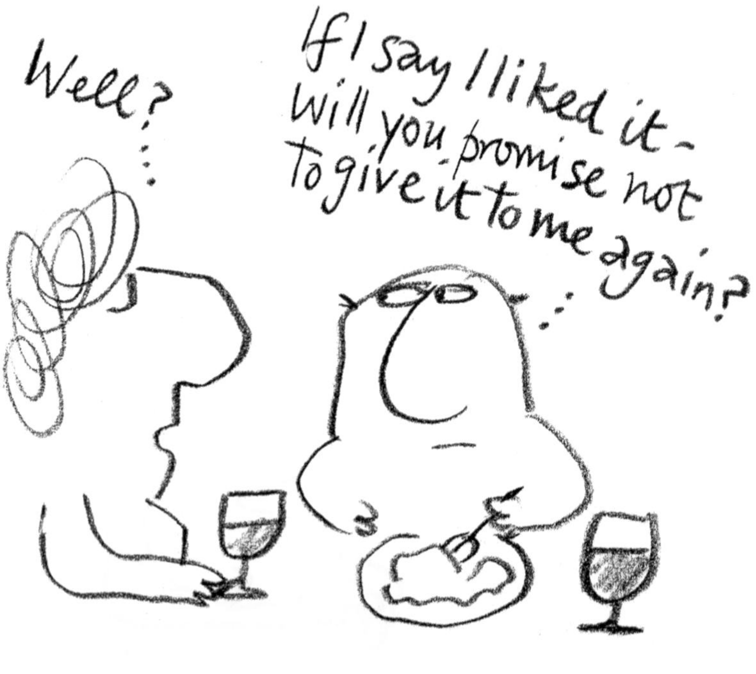
Well?
If I say I liked it - will you promise not to give it to me again?

What do you REALLY want?
I want you to know without my telling you..

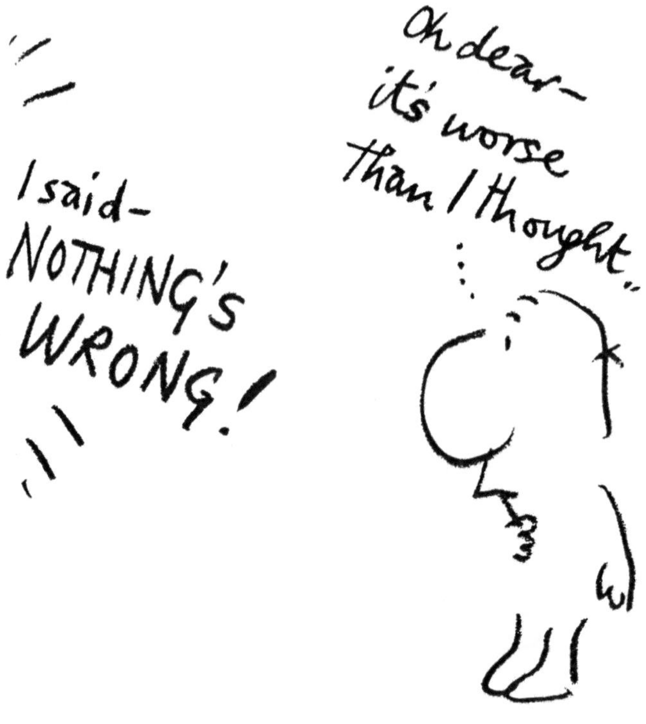
I said-
NOTHING'S
WRONG!
Oh dear-
it's worse
than I thought..

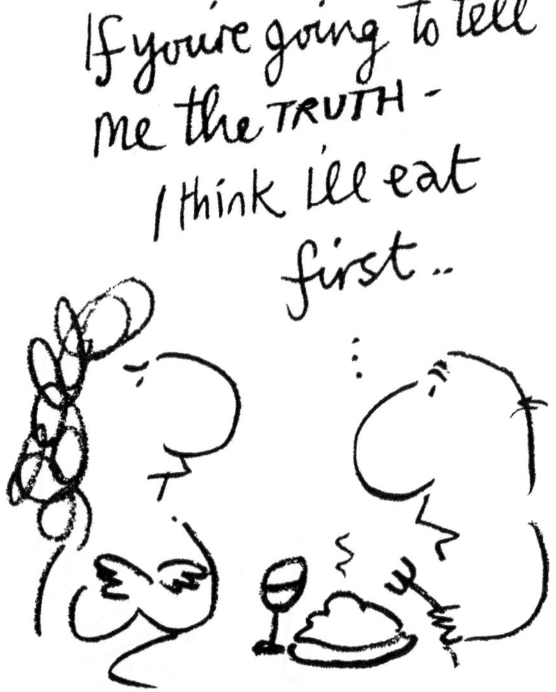
If you're going to tell
me the TRUTH -
I think I'll eat
first..

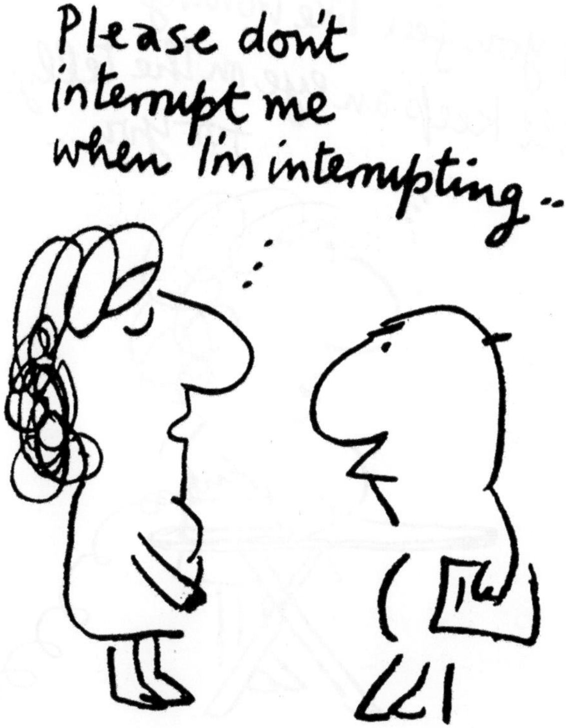
Please don't
interrupt me
when I'm interrupting..

If you feel like ironing -
I'll keep an eye on the telly
for you...

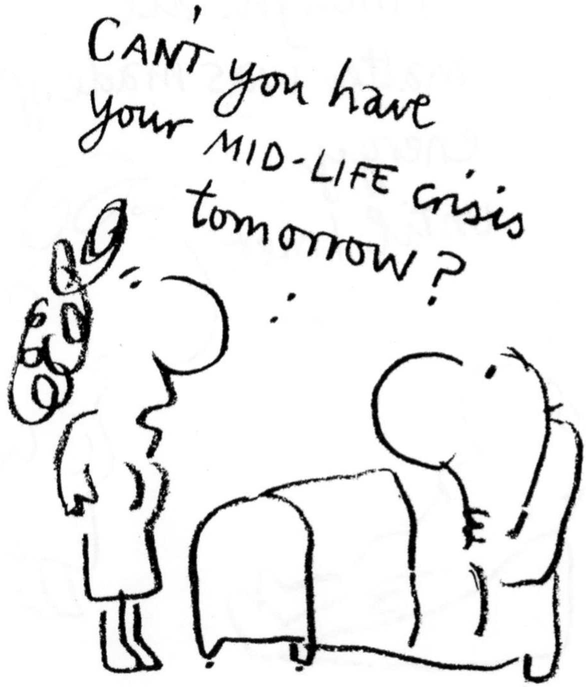
CAN'T you have
your MID-LIFE crisis
tomorrow?

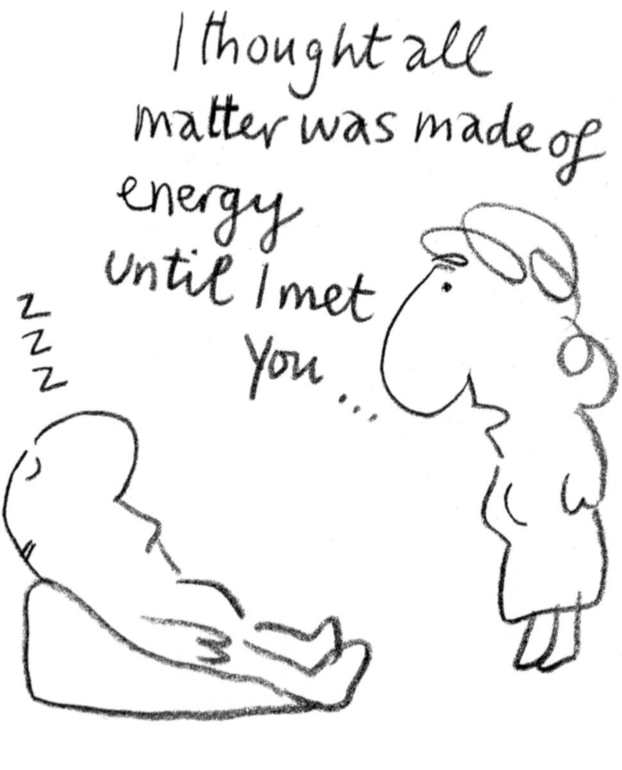
I thought all matter was made of energy until I met you . . .
ZZZ

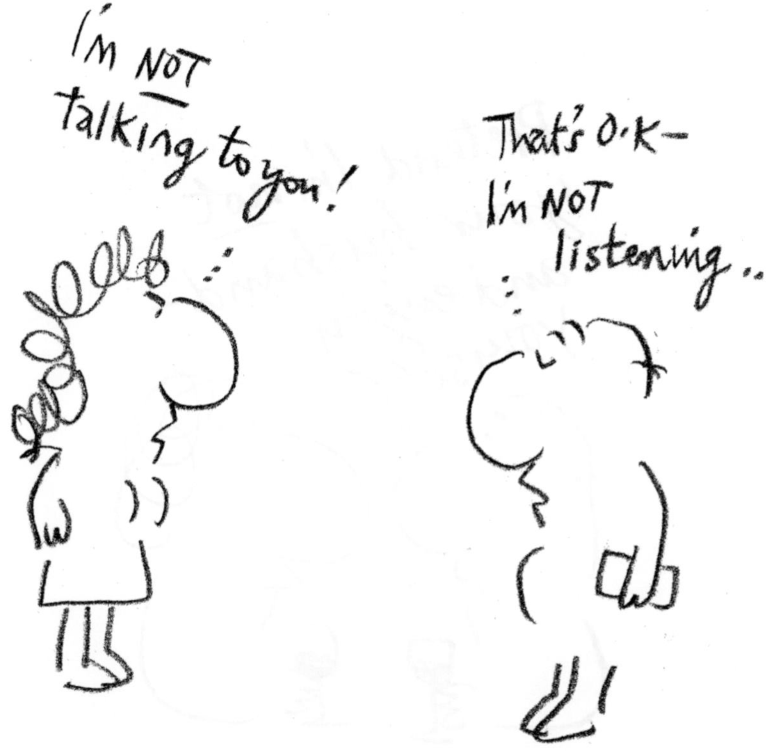
I'm NOT talking to you!
That's O.K— I'm NOT listening..

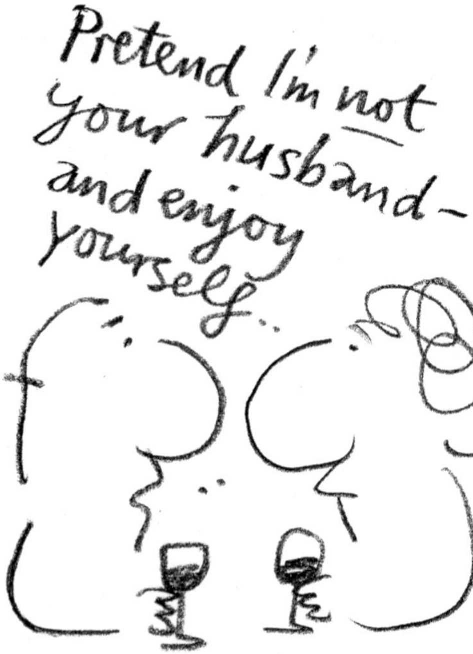
Pretend I'm not your husband - and enjoy yourself...

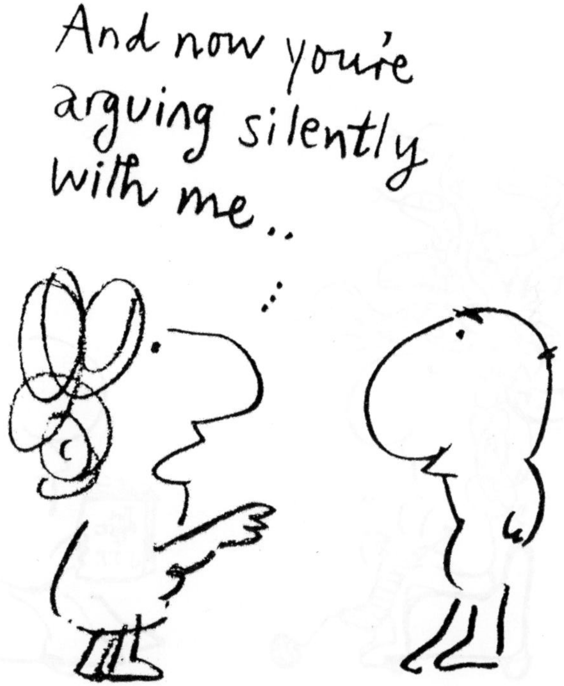
And now you're arguing silently with me...

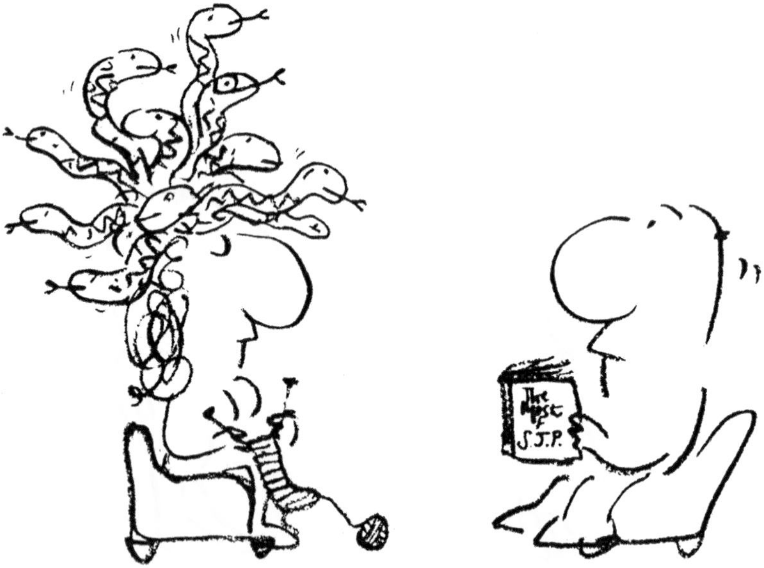
S.J.P.

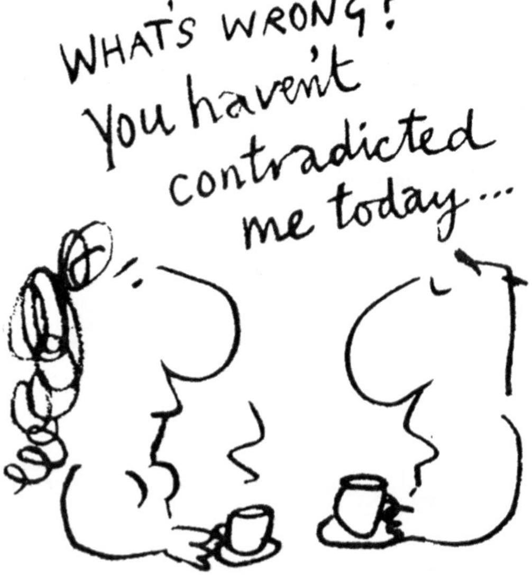
WHAT'S WRONG?
You haven't
contradicted
me today...

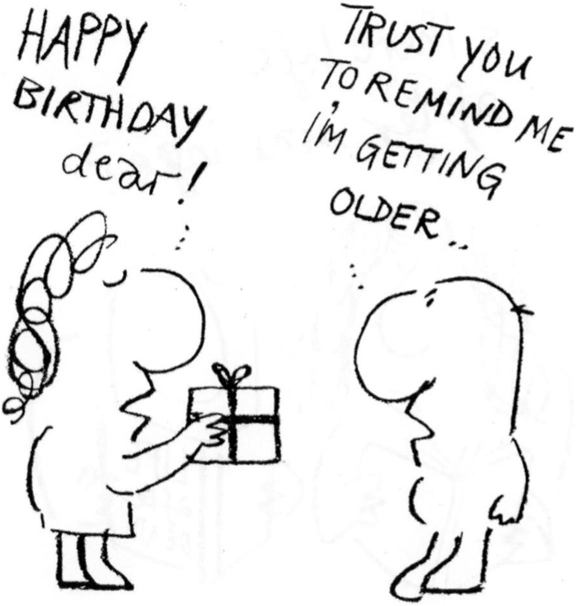
HAPPY BIRTHDAY dear!
TRUST YOU TO REMIND ME I'M GETTING OLDER..

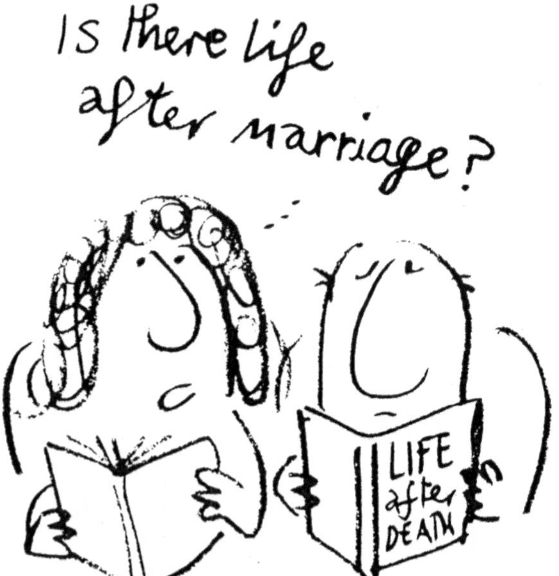
Is there life
after marriage?
LIFE
after
DEATH

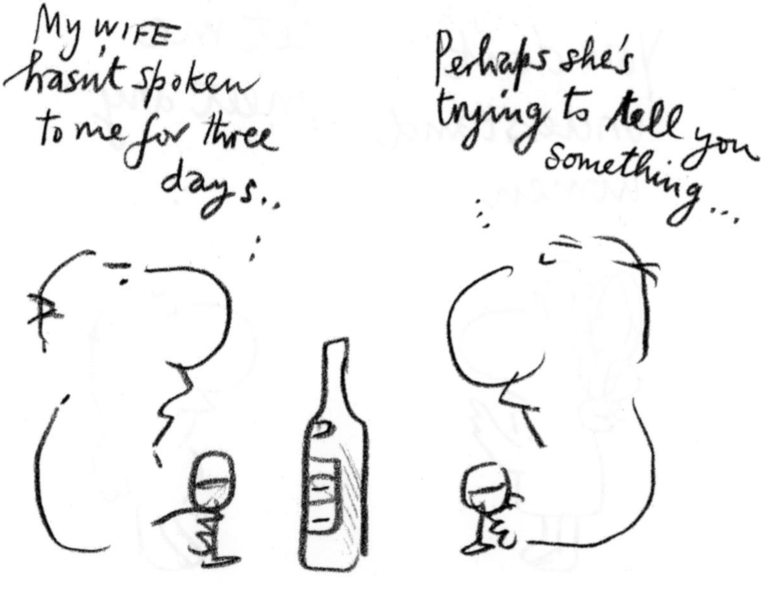
My WIFE hasn't spoken to me for three days...
Perhaps she's trying to tell you something...

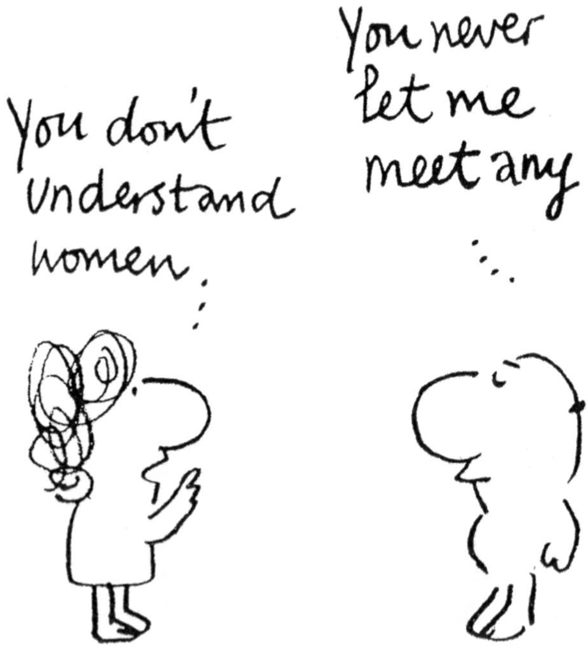
You don't understand women
You never let me meet any

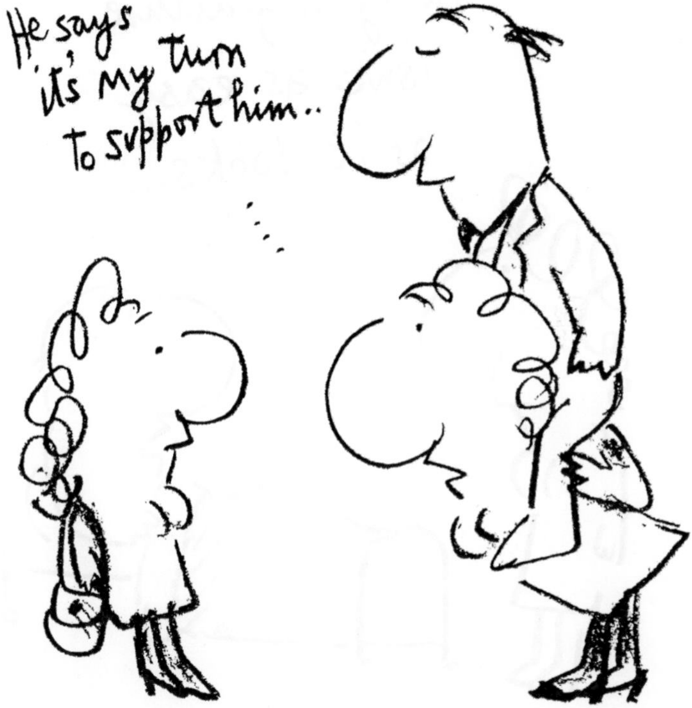
He says
it's my turn
to support him...

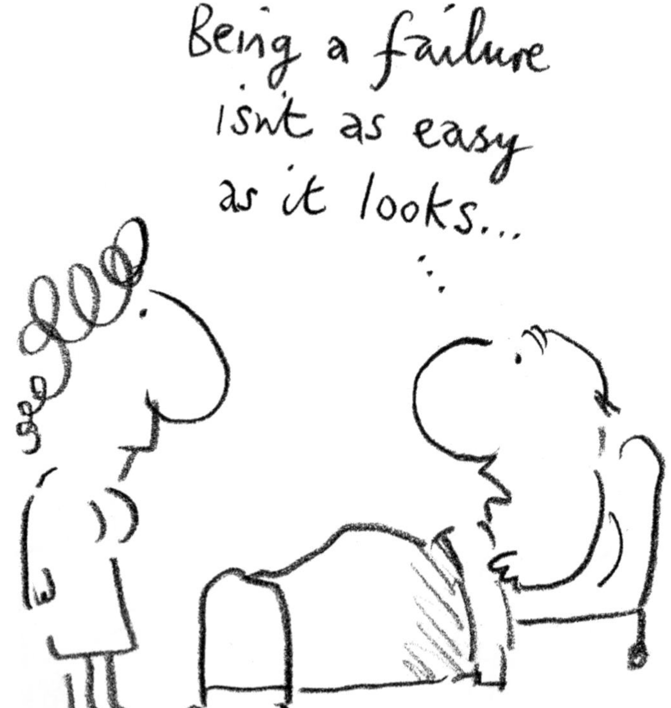
Being a failure isn't as easy as it looks...

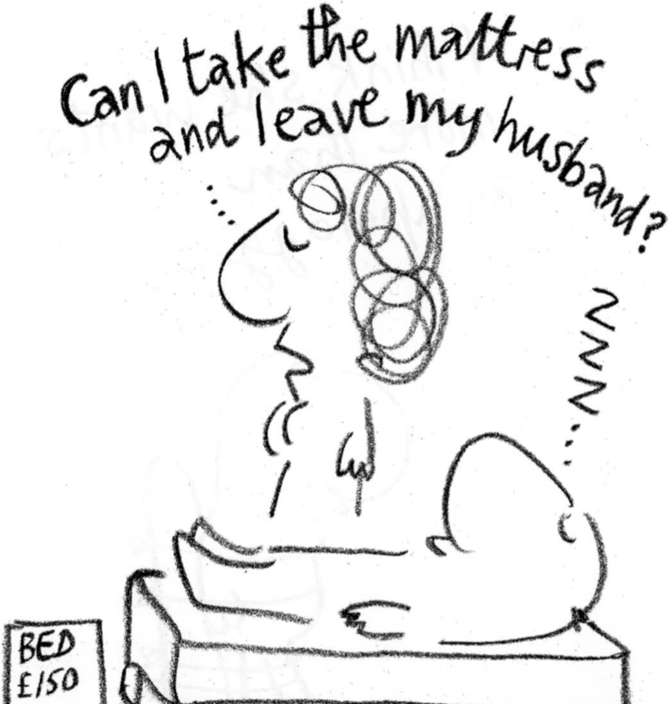
Can I take the mattress and leave my husband?
ZZZ...
BED £150

I think she wants
more than
an apology..

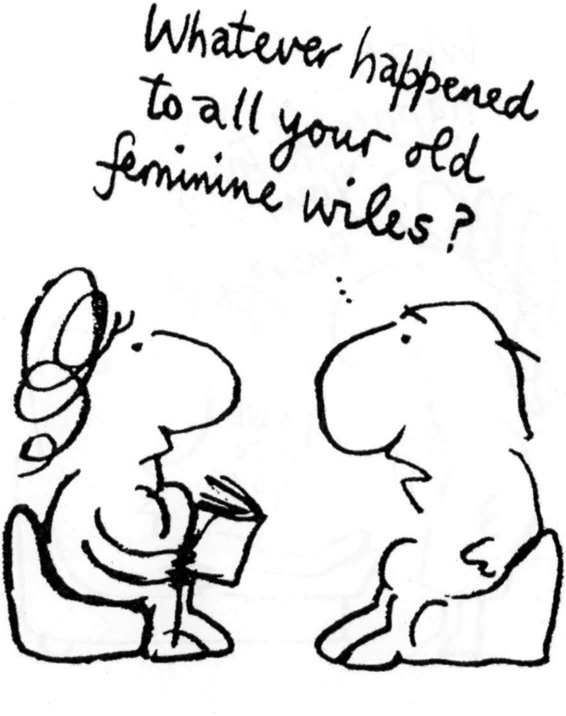
Whatever happened to all your old feminine wiles?

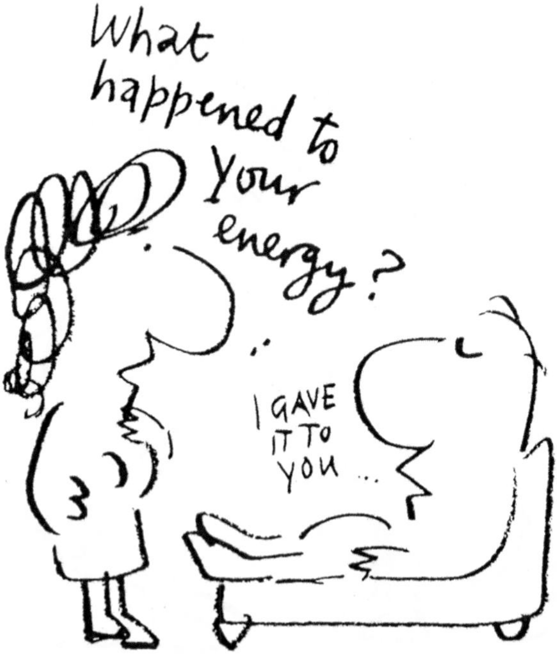
What happened to your energy?
I GAVE IT TO YOU ...

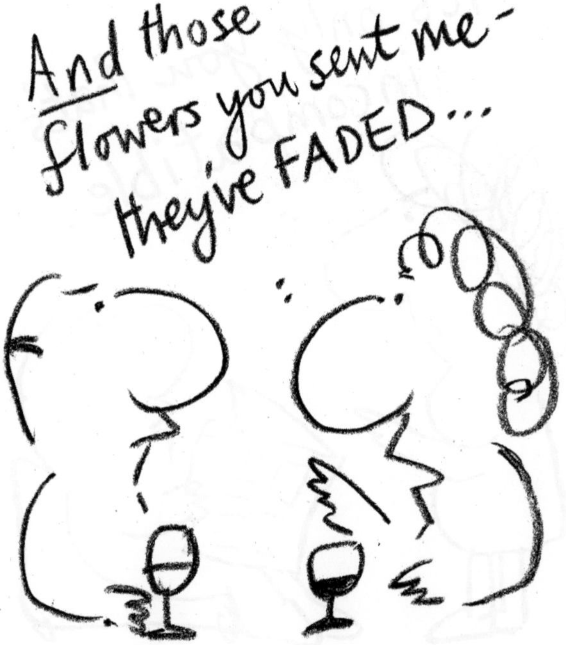
And those flowers you sent me - they've FADED...

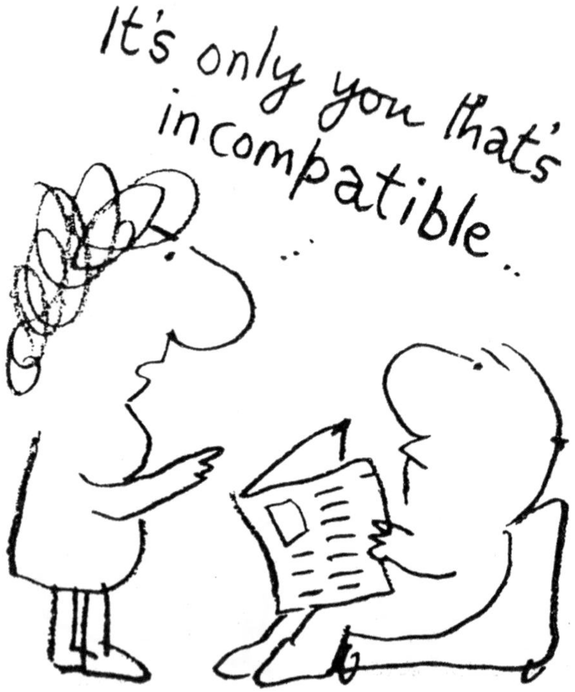
It's only you that's incompatible...

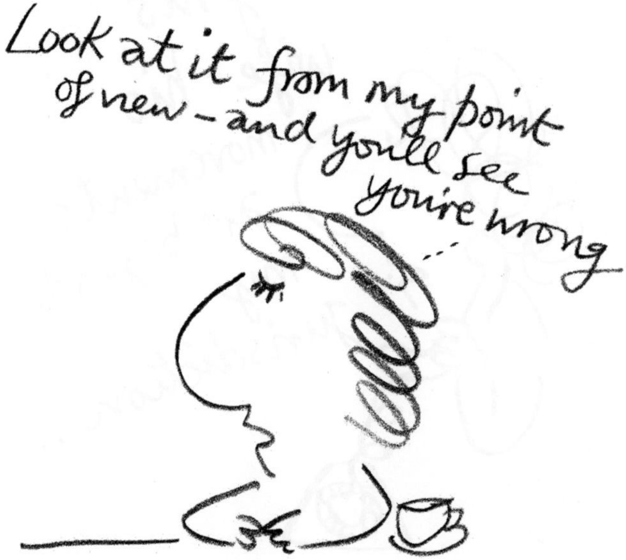
Look at it from my point of view - and you'll see you're wrong

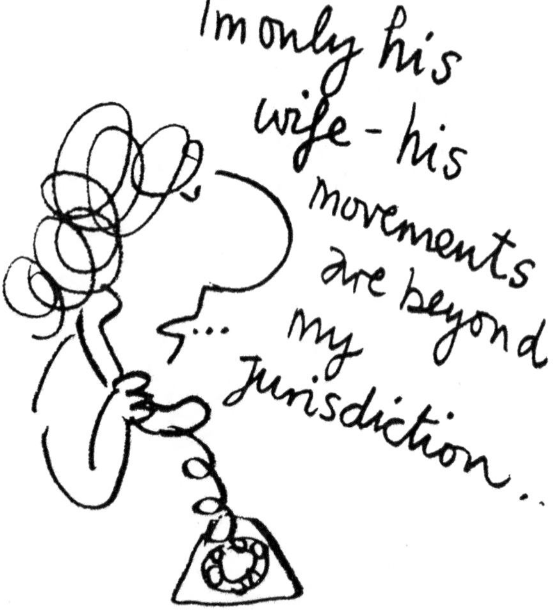
I'm only his wife - his movements are beyond my jurisdiction..

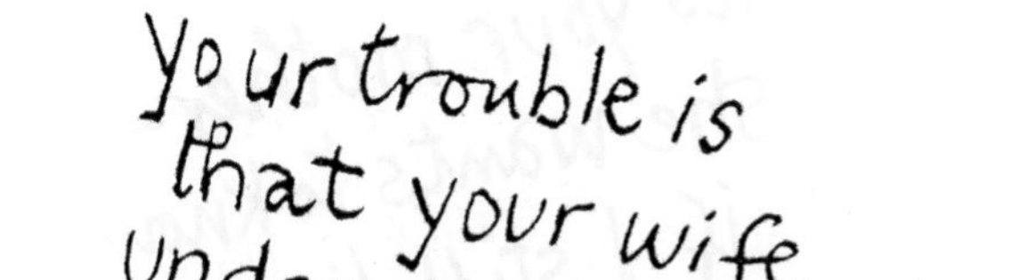
your trouble is
that your wife
understands you...

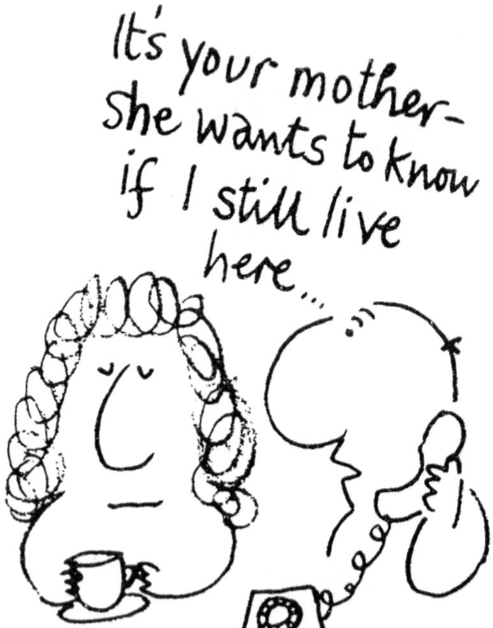
It's your mother-
She wants to know
if I still live
here....

I will LOVE you forever and ever – so long as we don't have to see so much of each other...

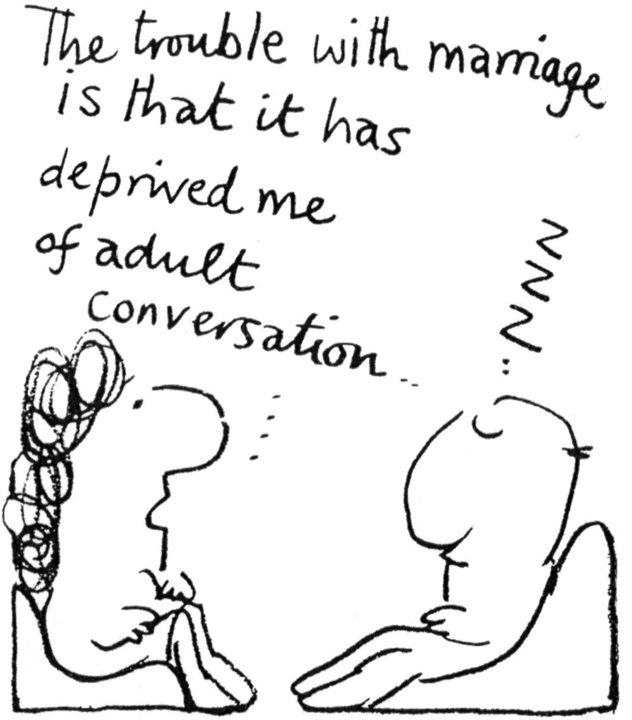
The trouble with marriage is that it has deprived me of adult conversation
ZZZ

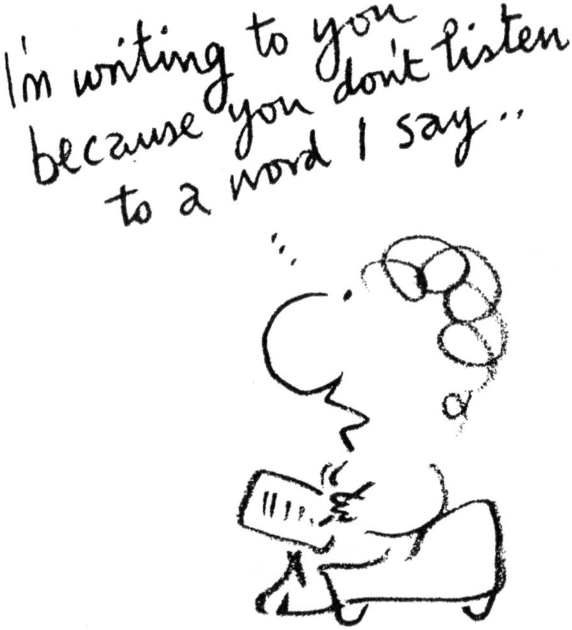
I'm writing to you
because you don't listen
to a word I say..

I've got no subconscious
resentment against you —
it's all conscious...

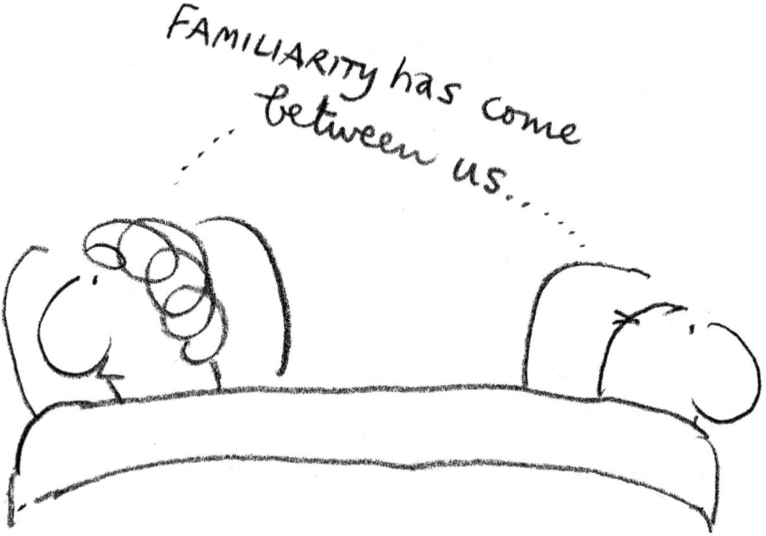
FAMILIARITY has come between us......

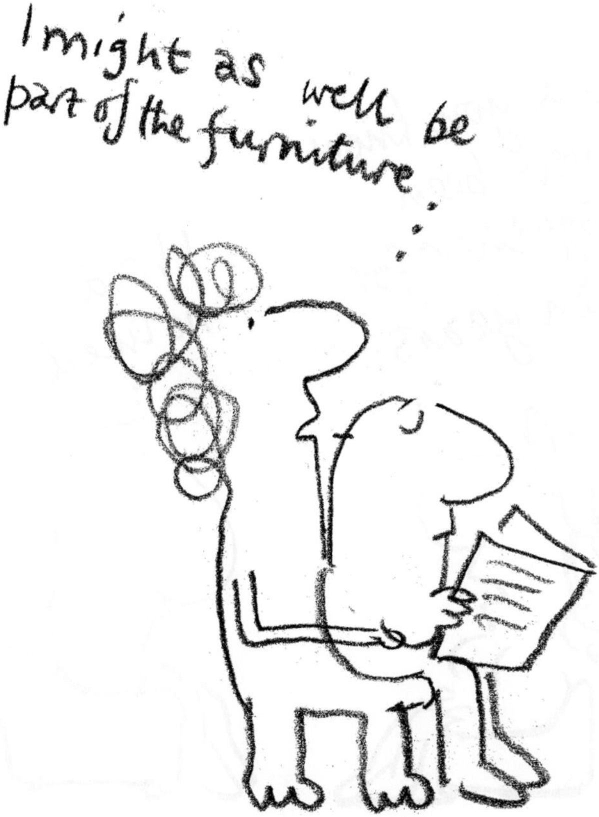
I might as well be part of the furniture...

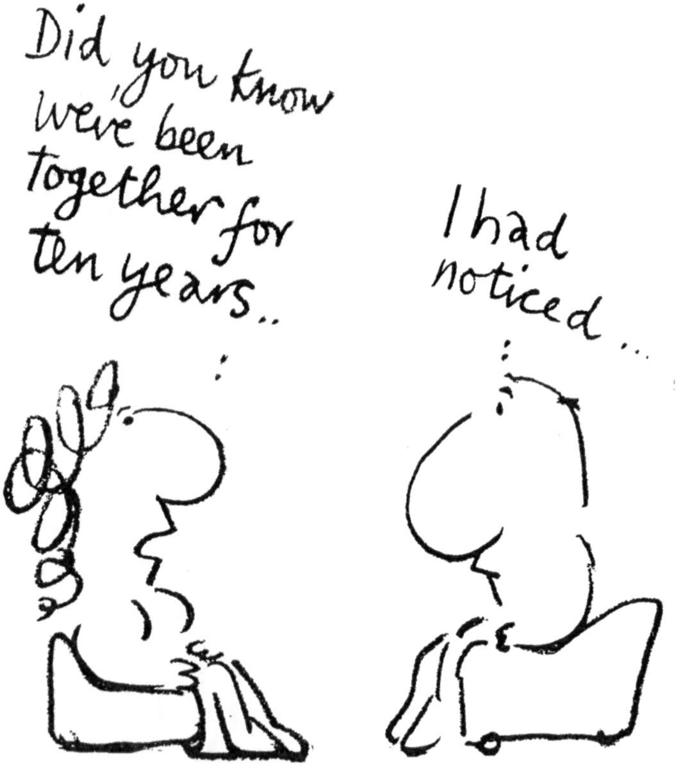
Did you know we've been together for ten years..
I had noticed...

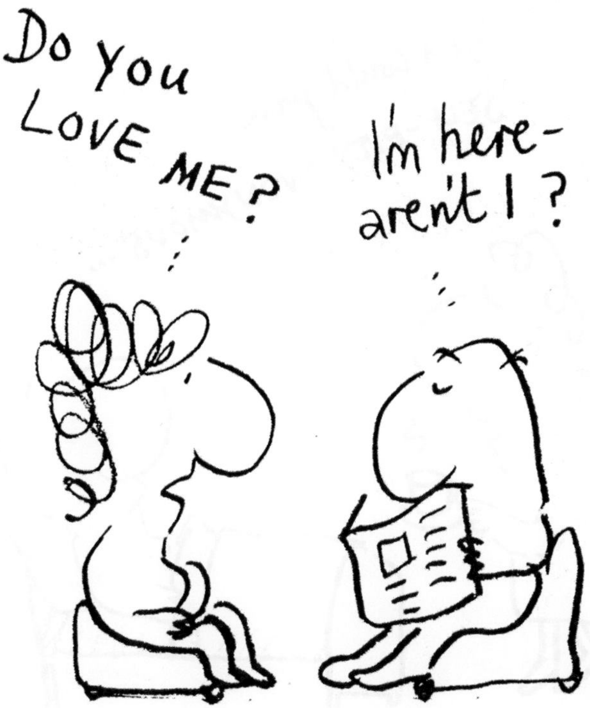
Do you LOVE ME?
I'm here-aren't I?

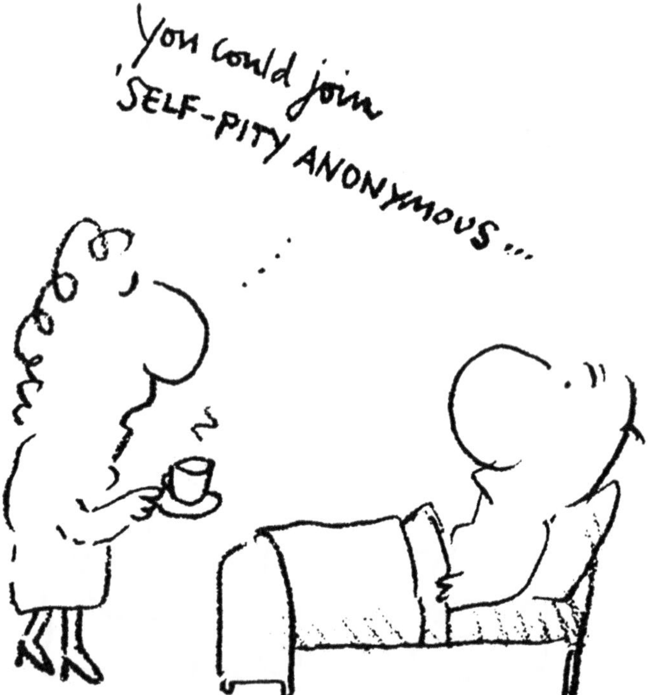
You could join
'SELF-PITY ANONYMOUS ...

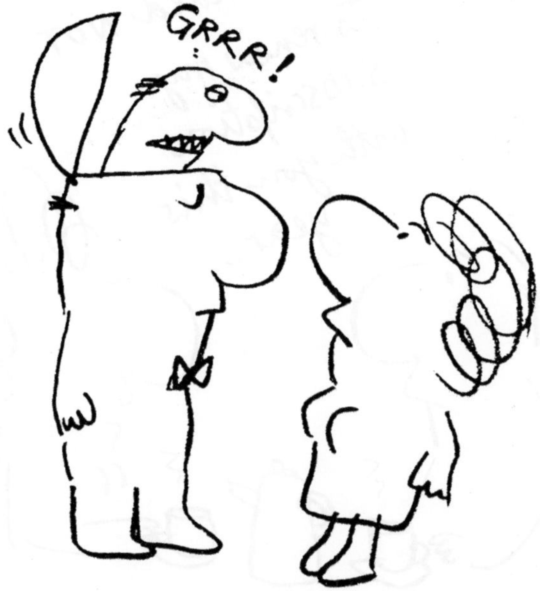
GRRR!

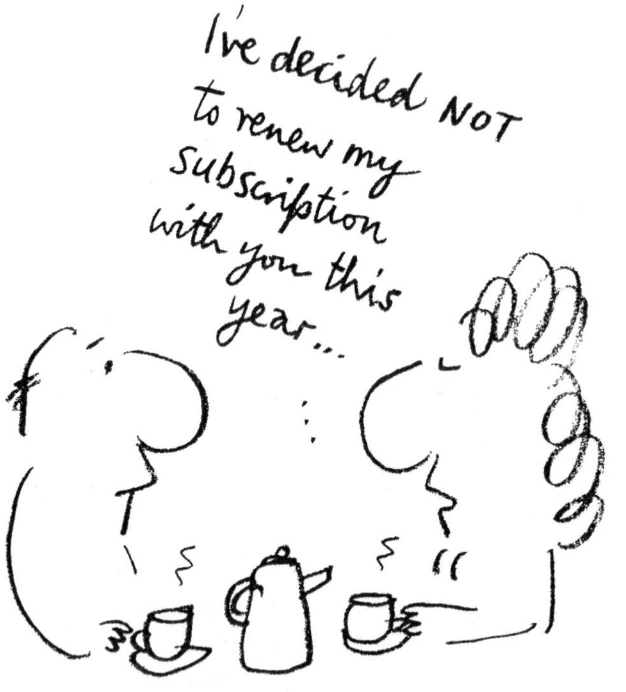
I've decided NOT to renew my subscription with you this year...

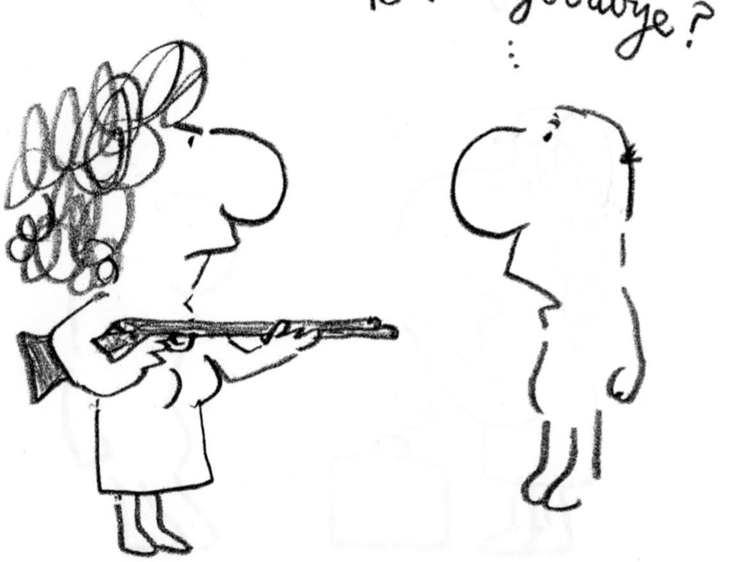
Is this goodbye?

If you're so perfect -
why am I leaving?

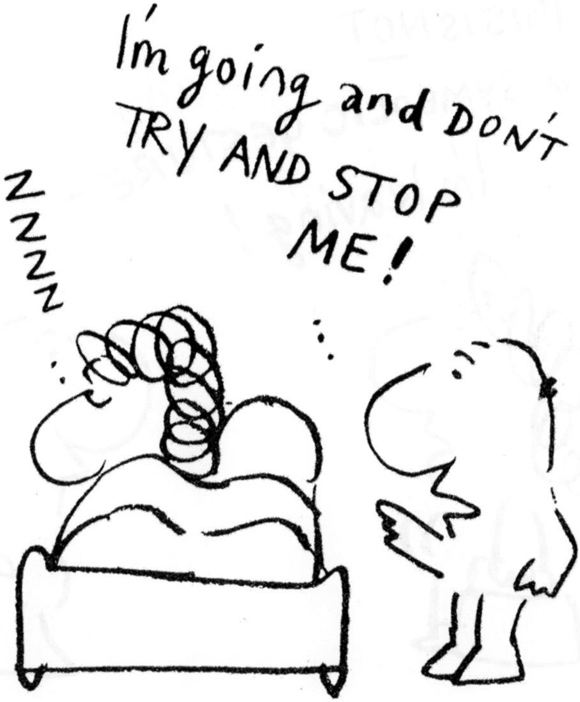
I'm going and DON'T TRY AND STOP ME!
ZZZZ

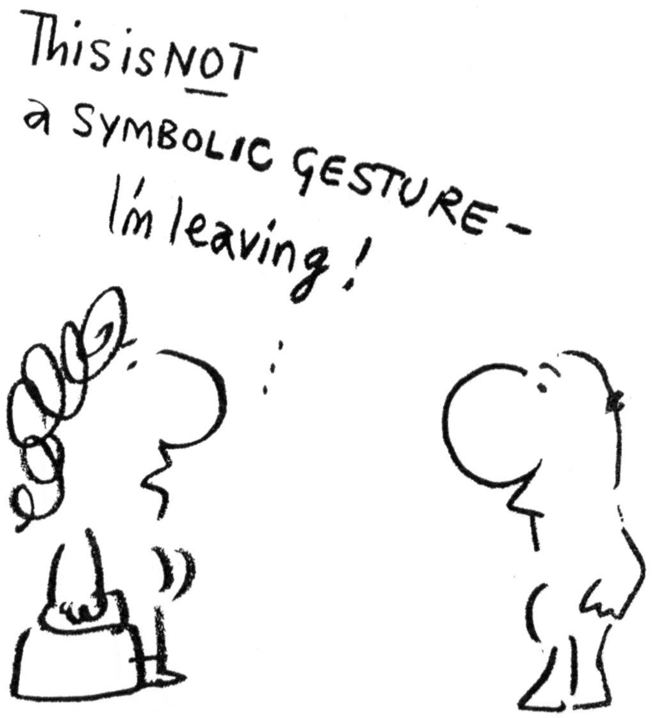
This is NOT a SYMBOLIC GESTURE - I'm leaving!

I seem to bring out the lawyer in a woman...

But it's my turn
to leave you .

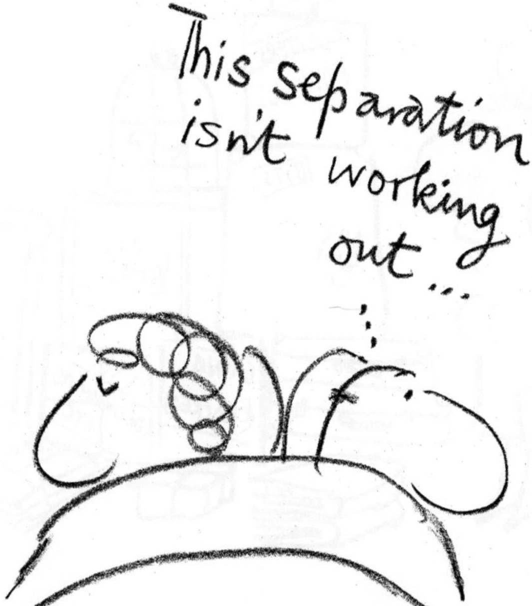
This separation isn't working out...

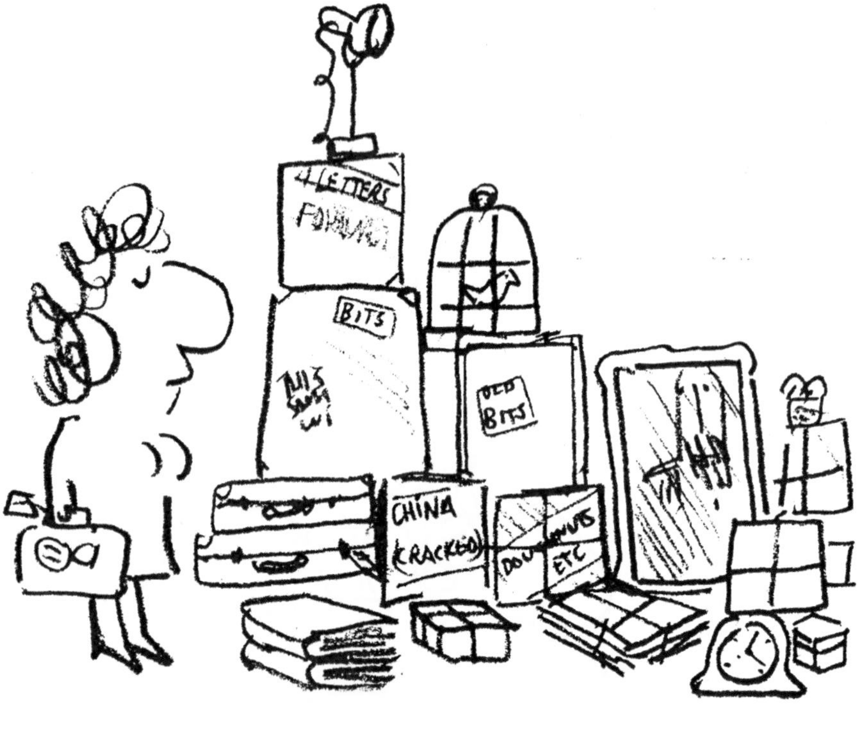
LETTERS
BITS
OLD BITS
CHINA
(CRACKED)
ETC

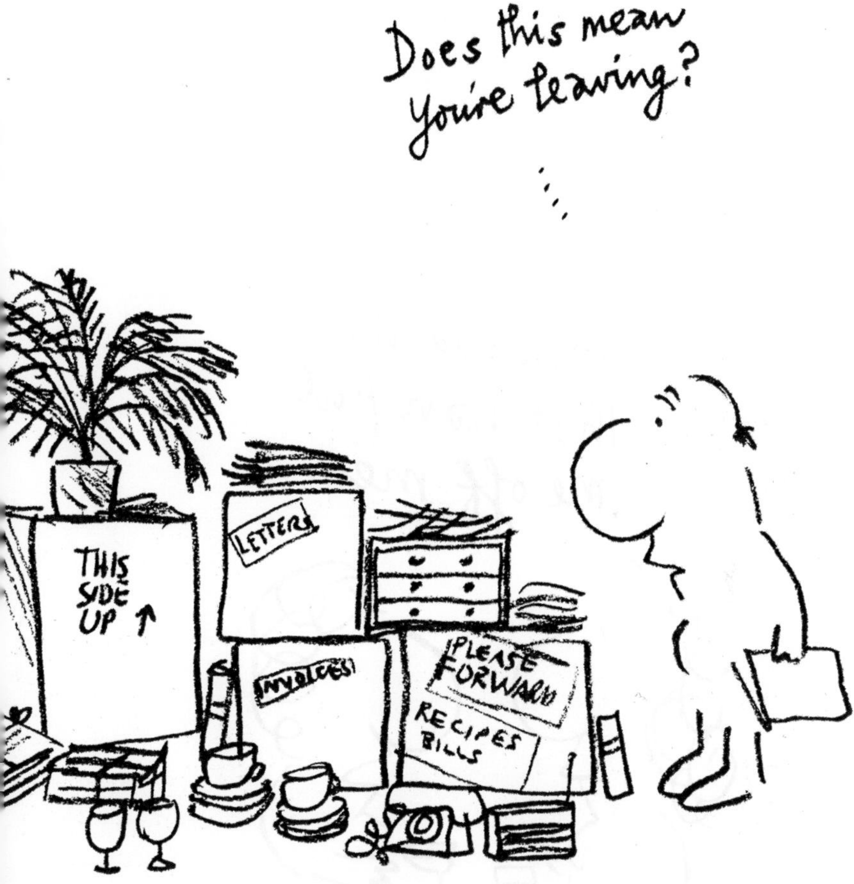
Does this mean you're leaving?
THIS SIDE UP
LETTERS
INVOICES
PLEASE FORWARD
RECIPES BILLS

it's husbands
that have put
me off men..

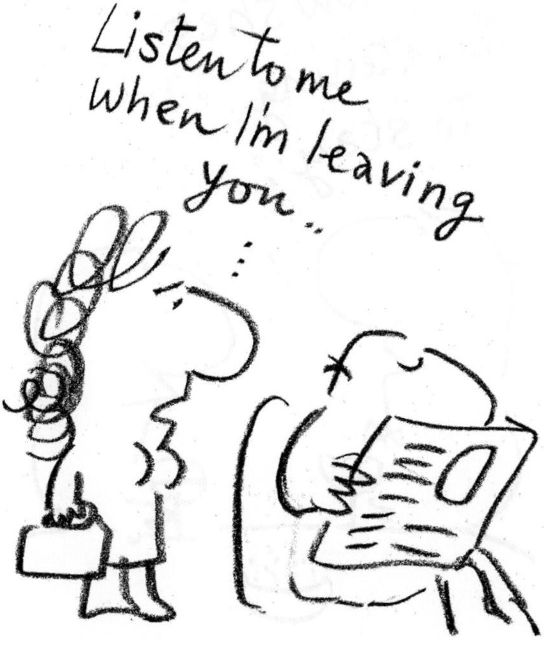
Listen to me
when I'm leaving
you..

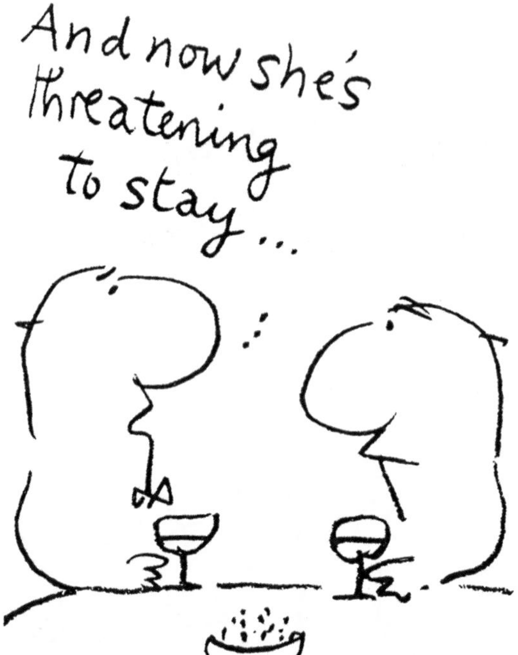
And now she's threatening to stay...

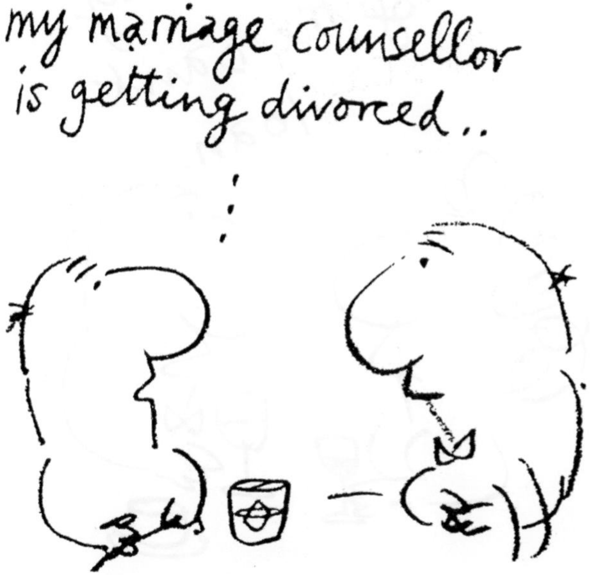
my marriage counsellor
is getting divorced..

I got custody
of the bank
loan...

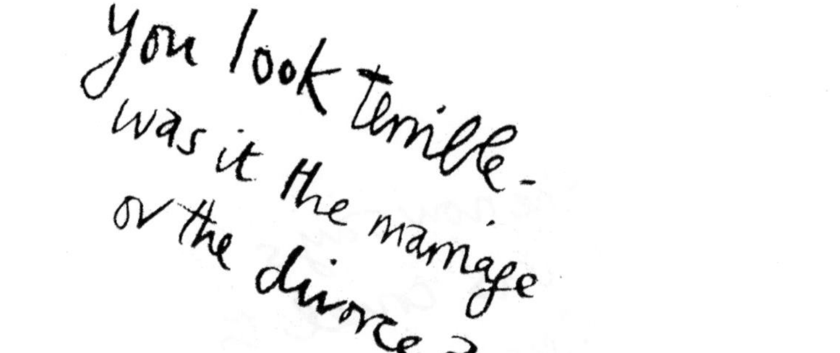
You look terrible -
was it the marriage
or the divorce?
BOTH.

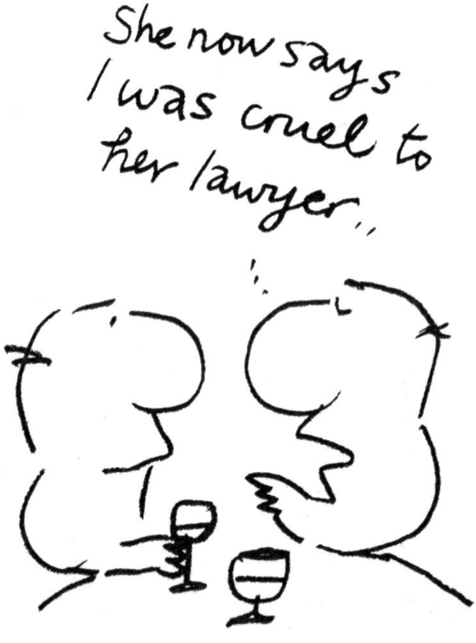
She now says
I was cruel to
her lawyer...

Will you be able to support a second wife in the style to which your first wife is accustomed?

We're going to rent
a villa with my kids,
his kids, and our
kids – to get away
from it all ..

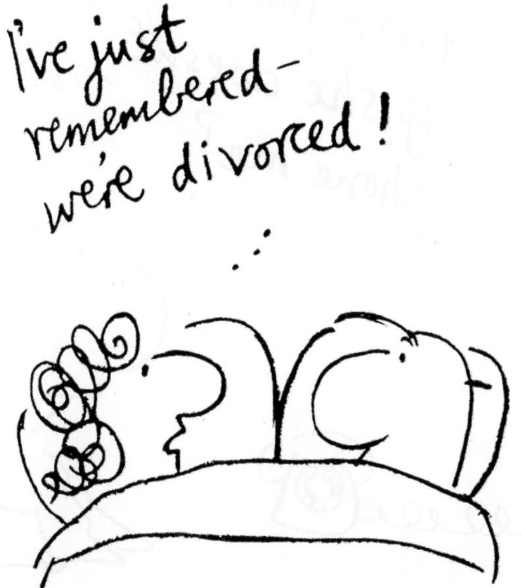
I've just
remembered-
we're divorced!

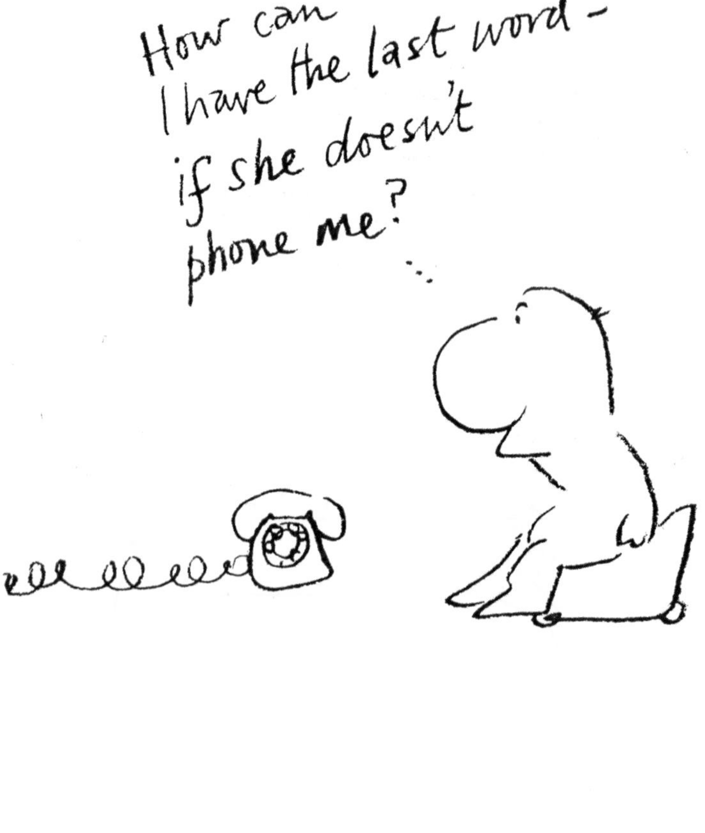
How can
I have the last word -
if she doesn't
phone me?

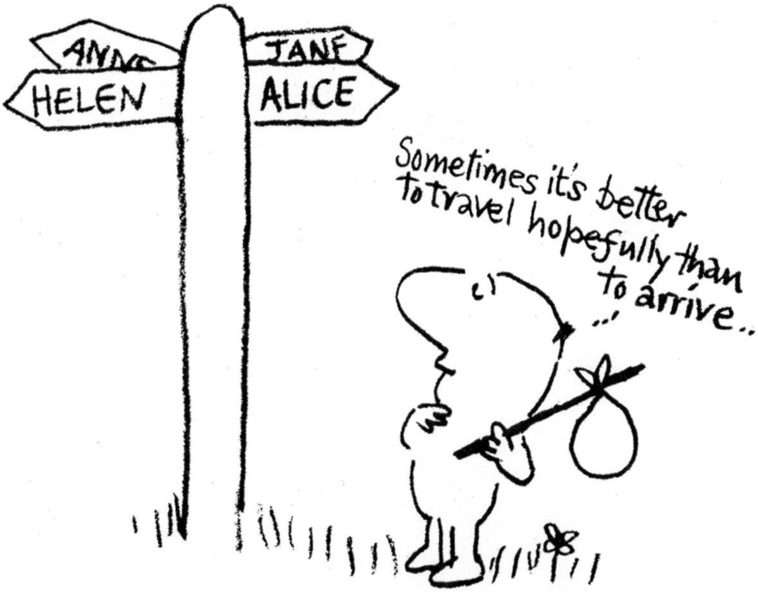
ANNE
JANE
HELEN
ALICE
Sometimes it's better to travel hopefully than to arrive...

Mel Calman was born in North London in 1931 into a middle-class Jewish family. During the war he was evacuated to Cambridge, where he won a scholarship to the Perse School. He then attended St Martin's School of Art, where he produced the college magazine – with fellow student Len Deighton who substituted his own cover design for Mel's. 'You could see *he* was destined for success,' Mel said admiringly. Of himself, he realised: 'I had no natural facility, so I had to develop the rest of my skills, and that led me to living by my wits.'

After art school came National Service, during which he failed basic training due to his inability to climb ropes, but was eventually let through because they needed an Education Sergeant, a post that came with separate accommodation, freeing him from the barracks and 'the smell of other men's socks'.

In 1956, he got his first commission, a Miles Davis album cover for a client so short-sighted he had to have the design described to him. Then in 1957 came regular work, providing daily 'column-fillers' – no more than one inch wide – for the Daily Express. He got married the same day, but didn't like to ask for any time off in case they changed their minds and gave the job to somebody else.

Mel's unique voice first surfaced with the creation of *Bed-Sit* in the Sunday Telegraph in 1962. Here, the little man that was to be his trade-mark first expressed the singular blend of hope and pessimism that infused all his later work. That year, he also produced his first book, *Through the Telephone Directory with Mel Calman*, later followed by *Calman & Women, My God* (a favourite of Archbishop Desmond Tutu), *Couples, But It's My Turn To Leave You, It's Only you that's Incompatible, Calman at the Royal Opera House, Dr Calman's Dictionary of Psychoanalysis, How About a Little Quarrel Before Bed?* and others. His autobiography was called *'What Else Do You Do?'* after the question he claimed he was most often asked at parties.

In 1969, by then drawing regularly for The Sunday Times, he was invited to draw a cartoon on the front page, a fixture that continued for 14 years. And despite the intense rivalry between the two papers, he also joined The Times from 1979, becoming as familiar a part of the front page as the masthead itself.

In 1970, Mel opened The Workshop – later The Cartoon Gallery. Shows by rising stars such as Posy Simmonds and Quentin Blake, as well as painters and illustrators like Michael Foreman and Sir Hugh Casson, helped to make it not only an informal support system for artists, but a gallery 'that people weren't too intimidated to walk into'.

His prodigious output also included an annual full colour picture feature for the Sunday Times on the Cannes Film Festival, cartoon specials on the Edinburgh Festival, countless book covers for other writers, a documentary for BBC about his ambivalent relationship with God – 'I'm not sure I believe in him, but I don't want him to hear me saying that' – and a film for the 'Holiday' programme about Barcelona. His legacy includes the Cartoon Museum in London, which he co-founded. He died, aged 62, on 10th February 1994.